**W9-BOL-881**

Pebble® Plus

Monkeys

Mandrill Monkeys

by Cecilia Pinto McCarthy

Consulting Editor: Gail Saunders-Smith, PhD

Consultant: Lori Perkins
Vice President of Collections, Zoo Atlanta

CAPSTONE PRESS
a capstone imprint

Pebble Plus is published by Capstone Press,
1710 Roe Crest Drive, North Mankato, Minnesota 56003
www.capstonepub.com

Library of Congress Cataloging-in-Publication Data
Pinto McCarthy, Cecilia.
Mandrills / by Cecilia Pinto McCarthy.
p. cm.—(Pebble plus. Monkeys)
Includes bibliographical references and index.
Summary: "Full-color photographs and simple text introduce mandrills"—Provided by publisher.
ISBN 978-1-62065-106-3 (library binding)
ISBN 978-1-4765-1080-4 (eBook PDF)
Mandrill—Juvenile literature. I. Title.
QL737.P93P56 2013
599.8'6—dc23   2012024130

Editorial Credits
Jeni Wittrock, editor; Bobbie Nuytten, designer; Svetlana Zhurkin, media researcher; Eric Manske, production specialist

Photo Credits
Corbis: Anup Shah, 13, 21; Getty Images: Anup Shah, 7, 9; Minden Pictures: JH Editorial/Cyril Ruoso, 17; Nature Picture Library: Fiona Rogers, 11, 19; Newscom: ANP/Vidiphoto, 15; Shutterstock: Cloudia Newland, cover, 1, Kitch Bain, 5, lantapix, 6 (left)

Note to Parents and Teachers

The Monkeys set supports science standards related to life science. This book describes and illustrates mandrill monkeys. The images support early readers in understanding the text. The repetition of words and phrases helps early readers learn new words. This book also introduces early readers to subject-specific vocabulary words, which are defined in the Glossary section. Early readers may need assistance to read some words and to use the Table of Contents, Glossary, Read More, Internet Sites, and Index sections of the book.

Printed in the United States of America in North Mankato, Minnesota.
092012   006933CGS13

Table of Contents

Colorful Monkeys 4

At Home in the Forest 8

Finding Food 10

Family Life 12

Monkey Talk 16

Staying Safe 20

Glossary 22

Internet Sites 23

Read More 23

Index 24

Colorful Monkeys

Mandrills are colorful monkeys.
They have red noses, blue
cheeks, and orange beards.
Even their bottoms are blue
and red.

Mandrills are the world's largest monkeys. Males weigh about 55 pounds (25 kilograms). Females are smaller. They are about 29 lbs (13 kg).

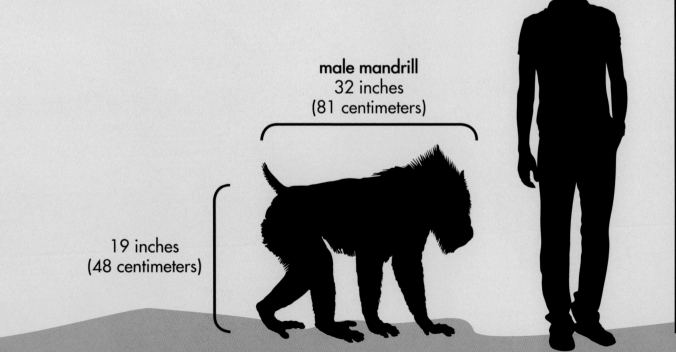

6 feet
(183 cm)

male mandrill
32 inches
(81 centimeters)

19 inches
(48 centimeters)

At Home in the Forest

Mandrills live in west-African rain forests. During the day, mandrills search for food. At night, they sleep safely in the trees.

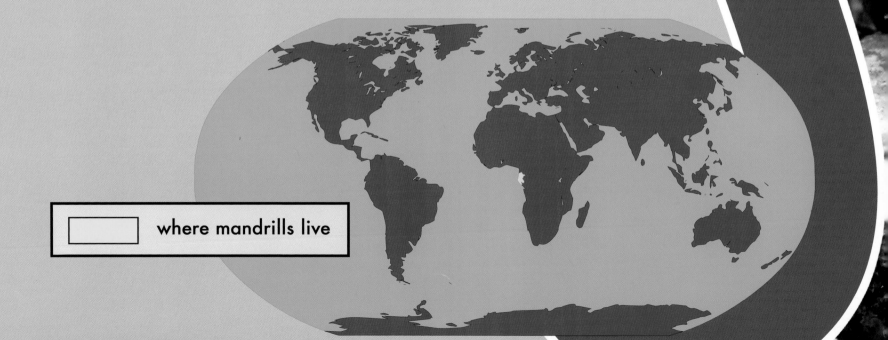

where mandrills live

Finding Food

Mandrills eat fruit, leaves, and bugs. They gobble roots, seeds, and mushrooms. Their cheeks have big pouches for storing food.

Family Life

Mandrills live in groups called harems. The harem's leader is the largest male. The females and babies are protected by the leader.

Female mandrills have a baby
once every two years.
Newborns have black fur and
pink skin. The babies cling
tightly to their mothers' bellies.

Monkey Talk

Mandrill harems are noisy. Mandrills grunt, roar, crow, and scream. Making noise helps mandrills find each other in the thick forest.

Mandrills show how they feel with their bodies. They smile to say hello. Angry mandrills slap the ground. Males show their teeth to scare enemies.

Staying Safe

Leopards, eagles, and people
hunt and eat mandrills.
Mandrills hide to stay safe.
They live about 20 years.

Glossary

beard—hair that grows around the mouth and chin

cling—to hold tightly to something

harem—a group of mandrills

pouch—a pocketlike fold of skin

protect—to keep safe

rain forest—a thick forest where a great deal of rain falls

store—to keep for later

Read More

Bodden, Valerie. *Monkeys*. Amazing Animals. Mankato, Minn.: Creative Education, 2010.

Monkeys. DK Readers. New York: DK Publishing, 2012.

Spilsbury, Louise. *Baboon*. Grassland Animals. Chicago: Heinemann Library, 2011.

Internet Sites

FactHound offers a safe, fun way to find Internet sites related to this book. All of the sites on FactHound have been researched by our staff.

Here's all you do:

Visit *www.facthound.com*

Type in this code: 9781620651063

Super-cool stuff!

Check out projects, games and lots more at
www.capstonekids.com

Index

babies, 12, 14

beards, 4

bottoms, 4

cheeks, 4, 10

colors, 4, 14

enemies, 18, 20

females, 6, 12, 14

foods, 8, 10

fur, 14

harems, 12, 16

hiding, 20

homes, 8

leaders, 12

life span, 20

males, 6, 12, 18

noses, 4

pouches, 10

size, 6

skin, 14

smiling, 18

sounds, 16

Word Count: 194

Grade: 1–2

Early-Intervention Level: 21